YOUR KNOWLEDGE HAS VALUE

Bibliographic information published by the German National Library:

The German National Library lists this publication in the National Bibliography; detailed bibliographic data are available on the Internet at http://dnb.dnb.de .

Imprint:

Copyright © 2009 GRIN Verlag
Print and binding: Books on Demand GmbH, Norderstedt Germany
ISBN: 9783668659520

This book at GRIN:

https://www.grin.com/document/414038

Maximilian Schott

Aus der Reihe: e-fellows.net stipendiaten-wissen

e-fellows.net (Hrsg.)

Band 2686

Threatened New Zealand Biodiversity. The Fate of the Possum

GRIN Verlag

GRIN - Your knowledge has value

Since its foundation in 1998, GRIN has specialized in publishing academic texts by students, college teachers and other academics as e-book and printed book. The website www.grin.com is an ideal platform for presenting term papers, final papers, scientific essays, dissertations and specialist books.

Visit us on the internet:

http://www.grin.com/

http://www.facebook.com/grincom

http://www.twitter.com/grin_com

Facharbeit des Kollegiaten

Maximilian Schott

im Leistungskurs Englisch

Kollegstufenjahrgang 2007/09

Threatened New Zealand Biodiversity -

The Fate of the Possum

Table of Contents

1. A Journey to New Zealand

When you ask people in Germany what they know about New Zealand, its beautiful and impressive landscape and nature will definitely be among the first things named. This unique beauty and purity of nature is probably one of the main reasons why so many students from all over the world dream of spending some time in Aotearoa, the land of the long white cloud, as it is called in Te Reo Maori.

So I felt very lucky when I got the chance to spend five months in Auckland on the North Island from January to July 2007, not only because I could experience a different way of life on the other side of the world, but also because it offered me the opportunity to explore 'godzone', God's own country, with its unique flora and fauna. The preservation of the country's beauty is one of the main topics of New Zealand's government policy and also a major issue in society.

As a visitor, you, most probably, will fairly soon get in touch with the strict rules that anyone entering the country has to obey, already before leaving the airplane. On my journey, all passengers on the plane from Sydney to Auckland were given a 'New Zealand Passenger Arrival Card' on which they had to answer questions about countries that they had visited within the last few years, goods that they were bringing in or whether they had recently stayed on a farm or had made hiking tours.

Fig. 1 *New Zealand Passenger Arrival Card*

That way, the Department of Conservation[*] wants to make sure that no animal products and no soil, which could be left on the soles of hiking boots or stick to any other outdoor equipment and which could possibly contain bacteria or parasites that would endanger New Zealand's endemic biota, are brought to the country. Therefore, all suitcases and bags are scanned twice for products like honey, eggs, feathers or meat. That is also why it takes much longer to get through customs at Auckland International Airport than it does e.g. in Frankfurt, Germany.

Now what is the reason why the Kiwis are so afraid of foreign animals and plants? Why are they doing everything to protect their endemic species by employing such a complex and expensive system of pest control, which, of course, is not limited to airports only, while at the same time being confronted with lots of crucial social problems to be solved for the solution of which the funds invested would also be badly required? May we even say the latter ones should be given priority? And what is it that makes nature on the green isles in the Pacific Ocean that unique and worth to be protected with such huge effort?

2. Biological Variety – Essential for Ecosystems

Taking a closer look at the importance and role of a healthy biodiversity, it becomes clear that the beauty which has to be preserved is just a small aspect compared to the multitude of natural services it provides[1] from which the most important are named below:

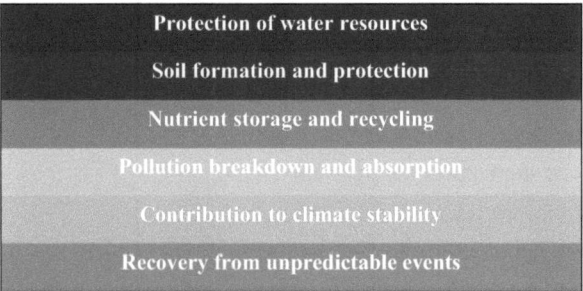

These processes and, moreover, the survival of a species is dependent if not mainly based on its interaction with others, which requires a broad range of species, i.e. a healthy biodiversity. Without the honey bee, the primary species that fertilises fruit-producing plants, "one-third of all our food – fruits and vegetables – would not exist"[2], which would have fatal consequences for all herbivores* and omnivores*. Being linked to carnivores by food web* connections, the decline of herbivores would result in a decline of carnivores. Summarised, that would mean, that the decline of honey bees would indirectly result in the decline of carnivores. A further example is the rising numbers of species suffering from predation if predator species are reduced, leading to rising numbers of predators with food resources becoming more and more abundant. Such relations exist all throughout the world's biota, making especially species which seem to be inconsiderable or unimportant at first glance the integral factor of ecosystem stability.

---

[1] Shah
[2] Shah

4

Considering all that, it is quite obvious, that the loss of single a species results in the decline and, at the same time, to the growth of other species, changing, in total, whole ecosystem compositions. An important point we should think about when deforesting huge parts of rainforest every day resulting in the decline of many species caused by the loss of habitat.

3. Aotearoa's Unique Biodiversity

An archipelago lying some 2,000 kilometres southeast of Australia in the southern Pacific Ocean, the New Zealand hotspot covers 270,197 km² on three main islands (North Island, South Island and Stewart Island) and several surrounding islands[3].

As it has been separated from other land masses for over 40 million years – when it split away from New Caledonia – it was possible for plants which were typical around the globe millions of years ago to survive, making the hotspot, nowadays, an "ancient life-raft"[4] which has, in addition, evolved a unique flora and fauna.

This chapter will show how this biota – which is one of a kind in the world – could develop, what it is like nowadays and how endemic species have been and still are suffering from globalisation in an invasive world.

3.1. Development of New Zealand's Unique Biota

As a land of varied landscapes – with rugged mountains, rolling hills and wide plains – and a wide range in latitude from subtropical to subantarctic[5], the country offers a huge variety of living conditions throughout the islands, thus allowing a multitude of animals and plants characterized by utmost different requirements to develop pretty well.

A key role in biodiversity distribution, however, plays the highly variable climate which ranges from subtropical, with warm, moist conditions throughout the year, for example on the Kermadec Islands, to cloudy, humid climate, with cool, wet winters and warm, usually dry summers on the Chatham Islands. Together with an annual rainfall varying from 12,000 millimetres on the western slopes of the Southern Alps, to less than 300 millimetres in their rainshadow areas on the east, the landscape of

---

[3] McGinley
[4] McGinley
[5] McGinley

the South Island is divided by the Southern Alps into rainforest on the west coast and wide plains on the east coast.

Not only the South Island, but also the North Island features many different ecosystems appealing to a variety of species. Going from north to south we will first encounter the huge Kauri forests in Northland which have been the reason why the island was once used by sealers and whalers as a base to restore their ships on their trips to the Antarctic.

The central North Island, however, is characterised by tectonic activities with mud pools reaching temperatures up to 800 °C at their ground, huge geysers and volcanoes like Mt. Ruhapehu. In contrast to the rich green rainforest and subtropical climate around Auckland, the barren region around Rotorua and especially the Tongariro National Park with its rocks and wide grasslands of yellow tussock seems to be bleak.

In total, that means that New Zealand's variety of ecosystems have made it possible for such a multitude of species with all kinds of requirements to evolve, resulting in the formation of today's impressive and often threatened biota.

3.2. New Zealand's Native Species Today

Just like the other fragments of ancient Godwanaland – Madagascar, Australia and New Caledonia – New Zealand features remarkable levels of endemism among plants, birds and reptiles.

Fig. 2 *Endemic Species Overview*

Taxonomic Group*	Species	Endemic Species	Percent Endemism
Plants	2,300	1,865	81.1
Mammals	10	3	30.0
Birds	195	86	44.1
Reptiles	37	37	100.0
Amphibians	4	4	100.0
Freshwater Fishes	39	25	64.1

As shown in the chart above, nearly 1,900 of about 2,300 species of plants are endemic and even 35 of New Zealand's plant genera are found nowhere else in the world. An example is the monotypic* genus *Desmoschoenus spiralis* or Pingao golden sand sedge*, a coastal plant which was used by the Maori in traditional building construction[6].

---

[6] McGinley

The fern *Loxoma cunninghamii* is one of the hotspot's 'living fossils' which constitutes, together with three species from Central America, the family *Loxomataceae*, whose closest relatives existed 60 million years ago. The hotspot has also one endemic family, the *Ixerbaceae*, which is represented by a single species (*Ixerba brexiodes*)[7].

In addition, 90 of 200 bird species which occur regularly in New Zealand are endemic, which is why five Endemic Bird Areas identified by BirdLife International occupy nearly the entire area of the country in order to protect them. The country also has 17 endemic bird genera and three endemic bird families (*Acanthisittidae*, *Aptery-gidae* and *Callaeidae*) and is, moreover, the only hotspot in the world to have an endemic bird order, represented by the flightless kiwi (*Apterygiformes*), which is also the national bird of New Zealand[8].

Although the country had a wide range of species in general, both land mammal species native to New Zealand were endemic bats (*Mysticina tuberculata* and *Mystacina robusta*), whereas endemic terrestrial mammals were completely non-existent before the arrival of humans. Their introduction following human settlement should proof to have fatal consequences on the hotspot's native biota.

Overall, we can say that New Zealand still is an 'ancient life-raft' with an impressive biodiversity including lots of species which exist nowhere else in the world, like e.g. the tuatara[*]. Unfortunately, lots of these species have become very rare or even endangered if not extinct, which is why people have to act in order to protect their country's beauty.

3.3. New Zealand in an Invasive World

3.3.1. Human Impacts

Although people came to New Zealand relatively late, i.e. about 600-800 years ago, human impact on the land and natural ecosystems has always been extensive. The first great impact was from hunting, fishing and gathering,

Fig. 3 *Model of the flightless Moa with Haast's Eagle on top at Te Papa Tongarewa, Wellington*

---

[7] McGinley
[8] McGinley

which caused the extinction of native bird species such as the giant moa and the Haast's Eagle[9], "the largest eagle to have ever lived"[10].

An even greater threat to the native biodiversity of New Zealand, however, was the introduction of invasive alien species[11]. Apart from seals and bats, all other terrestrially-breeding mammals in New Zealand are immigrants to this land which were introduced by humans. The first mammals to be introduced to the country were kuri, a dog (*Canis familiaris*), and kiore, the Polynesian rat (*Rattus exulans*) which Polynesian immigrants brought with them on their ships. Nowadays, the kuri is gone and the kiore, itself the victim of competition from subsequent introductions of other species, is restricted mainly to offshore islands[12].

Although the impact of those first alien mammalian species had already been fatal as it had resulted in the decline of numbers of native species, the most lethal invasion of mammals occurred with the arrival of Europeans at the end of the 17th century, who liberated everything from alpacas to zebras. Almost every one of the species that became established has left its destructive mark on the native New Zealand environment. Among the most important species liberated by Europeans were pigs (*Sus scrofa*), goats (*Capra hircus*) and several species of bovids, which were, like the goats, introduced during the 19th century as a food source for the young country's growing society.

Fig. 4 *Traditional New Zealand sheep farming*

Not only the bare introduction but also the treatment of alien species contributed to their success. Introduced sheep (*Ovis aries*), for example, were often put on unfenced

[9] Conservation International
[10] Haast's Eagle
[11] Conservation International
[12] Darby 142

range, which is the reason why the population of feral sheep, a danger to native flora, quickly became established and widespread[13].

Nevertheless, it were the mammals that Captain James Cook, the early sealers and settlers at the beginning of the 19th century introduced unintentionally that have had some of the most catastrophic effects on New Zealand's ecosystems. The Norway rat (*Rattus norvegicus*), the common ship rat (*Rattus rattus*), the house mouse (*Mus musculus*) – which is even able to kill lizards and has had major impact on New Zealand's native invertebrate fauna[14] – and also the ships' cats (*Felis cattus*) are probably the species that have to be mentioned, as they have managed to establish huge populations throughout the country[15].

Many cats were released by farmers from the mid to the late nineteenth century in an attempt to control the growing populations of the European rabbit (*Oryctolagus cunilungus*), which had been responsible for serious devastations to grazing land. For the same reason farmers demanded to import the rabbits' natural predators, like e.g. ferrets (*Mustela putorius*), stoats (*Mustela erminea*) and weasels (*Mustela nivalis*). Hence, from 1879 to 1886, thousands of ferrets, 592 weasels and 214 stoats were released only on the South Island at sites including Lake Wanaka, the Makarora and Wilkin Valleys, Lake Wakitipu and parts of Southland. Unfortunately, these mustelids* had little effect on the rabbit population, but by 1892 the damage weasels and stoats were causing to native birds, as they moved into the forests of Fiordland and the like, was becoming apparent[16].

The rabbit itself had been introduced to the country by James Cook in 1777, although the main reason for its spread certainly was the subsequent importation by the so-called Acclimatisation Societies, which organised releases on the North as well as on the South Island[17].

Founded from the early 1860s onwards, the main goal of the Acclimatisation Societies was the "introduction, acclimatisation and domestication of all innoxious animals, birds, fishes, insects, and vegetables whether useful or ornamental"[18] as is fixed in the Rules of the Acclimatisation Society of Auckland, stated at a meeting on 30 July, 1862. By stocking the country systematically with familiar animals and plants which had not existed there before, their purpose was to create a 'second

---

[13] Darby 142
[14] Darby 143
[15] Darby 144
[16] Darby 145
[17] Darby 144
[18] McDowall 19

9

Britain'. The only problem was that most of the species that they considered 'innoxious', like e.g. rabbits, deer, cats, pigs or brushtail possums turned out to be a serious threat to the native biota of their new country.

3.3.2. Alien Invasions – A One-Sided Battle

Overall, we can summarise that basically all introductions of foreign species have had far-reaching fatal effects on New Zealand's native flora and fauna. Although they occur all over the world, there are huge regional differences in the consequences biological invasions have on a country's biota. But why have, in New Zealand's case, those consequences been that disastrous?

The main reason for the devastating effects of alien biota on endemic species has been the "poor representation or absence of certain functional groups"[19], i.e. the absence of indigenous snakes, predatory terrestrial* mammals, colonial bees, wasps and ants during its formation. This circumstance has resulted in a "one-sided battle following human settlement between ecologically naive islanders and sophisticated continentals"[20]. One typical example is the absence of mammalian herbivores and the abundance of herbivorous birds like moas which had resulted in the development of avian-specific defences of plants against natural enemies. That is why large numbers of plants were sensitive to mammalian browsing following human settlement as they had not been used to it before and, therefore, had no defence against it. A similar problem occurred with a lot of native birds, like e.g. the kiwi. In absence of mammalian and snake predators, large flightless or weakly flighted birds could develop pretty well. Being confronted with exactly those predators now, they had no chance to survive[21]. These are just two examples out of a lot more, but they give us an idea of what was the main reason of the "one-sided battle"[22].

Secondly, the ephemeral nature of certain habitats in New Zealand over a glacial-interglacial cycle (e.g. lowland grasslands, cold tundra, warm-temperate forest) may have limited the degree to which indigenous species could adapt, which might have given an advantage to continental species that are specialists for such habitats. For instance, a number of cold-adapted continental trees that could grow well above the

---

[19] Allen 26
[20] Allen 26
[21] Allen 28
[22] Allen 26

New Zealand tree line may have the potential to exclude the indigenous tussocks and low shrubs currently growing there[23].

Finally, the total conversion of much of the lowland and montane New Zealand landscape into an open exotic grassland, different in basic ways to any existing in the past, has strongly affected the balance between islander and exotic. Burning and felling of dark, moist forests and their replacement with human-managed grass-lands have effectively created a drier, warmer and more fire-prone prairie or steppe environment with greatly elevated soil fertility which was essential for the upcoming agricultural society of early New Zealand[24]. Even nowadays, the difference between what New Zealand was like before the arrival of humans and what huge parts of it are like now is still visible if you look at the biota of one of the many national parks that cover most of the country, where the ancient rainforest is still prevailing.

Fig. 5 *Tussock grassland near Mt Ngauruhoe*   **Fig. 6** *Rainforest at Lake Tarawera*

Those three aspects combined, in the case of many indigenous birds, reptiles and giant invertebrates, have meant rapid extinction or reduction to small, protected enclaves. Although mammalian herbivore pressure has reduced many indigenous plants over wide areas, the overall influence has not been as fatal as on New Zealand's endemic fauna[25].

Summarizing all aspects mentioned before, we can say that New Zealand's discovery by humans was probably the worst thing that could possibly happen to its endemic biota. Not only habitat destruction, through deforestation, wetland drainage and ecosystem degradation, but rather the introduction of invasive alien species to

---

[23] Allen 28
[24] Allen 28
[25] Allen 26

the country has led to the extinction of 16 land birds, one endemic bat, one fish, at least a dozen invertebrates, and ten plants within a period of about 200 years[26]

4. Trichosurus Vulpecula – 'Keystone Aliens'

The Common Brushtail Possum (*Trichosurus Vulpecula*) was originally endemic to Australia. It is a solitary, nocturnal*, arboreal* marsupial weighing 2-4 kg and it is, despite of its cute appearance, probably the best example of the fatal influence that aliens can have on endemic species in New Zealand.

Fig. 7 *Brushtail Possum and baby*

The following pages will show how it was possible for an Australian animal to spread in New Zealand, its importance to and its influence on New Zealand's biota and how the Kiwis try to protect their native flora and fauna against the probably most important 'keystone alien'.

4.1. The Australian Brushtail Possum Invading New Zealand

The possum was introduced to New Zealand from eastern Australia and Tasmania in the mid-19th century[27]. First imported by Southlander Christopher Basstian in 1858 or even earlier at Riverton in 1837, the prime reason for the animals to be brought to the country was to establish a "valuable fur industry"[28]. Possum skins reached high prices at auctions and acclimatisation societies received a levy on each skin, which is probably the main reason why they decided to get involved with possums and started to bring stock from Victoria (grey possums) and Tasmania (black possums) to New Zealand. From then on, vigorous transfer and systematical importation to new areas as well as private liberations of possums continued until the 1920s when it became officially illegal[29].

Today, it is obvious that in the early years there was wide acceptance that having possums in New Zealand's forests was beneficial as the Wellington Society stated in 1892 that "the opossum need never be regarded as a pest in New Zealand"[30] and in Auckland's opinion the societies were "doing a great service to the country in

---

[26] McGinley
[27] Allen 265
[28] McDowall 358
[29] McDowall 358
[30] McDowall 359

stocking these large areas [...] with this valuable and harmless animal"[31]. Even when possums became more and more troublesome in orchards and gardens, biologist Harold Kirk who had been commissioned by the government to advise the impacts of possums in 1919, concluded that, whilst damage to orchards and gardens was indisputable, "the damage to New Zealand forests is negligible"[32]. He recommended that possums be released in all forest districts away from orchards and gardens as that way they would no longer represent any danger.

Fig. 8 *Possum introduction and subsequent distribution*

So, their release continued and by 1930 possums had been introduced into 450 locations around the country. But not only importation continued. Moreover, possums were protected until 1946, when they were officially declared an environmental pest and in 1947, all protection was removed[33]. The government

---

[31] McDowall 359
[32] Allen 266
[33] Possums

cancelled all restrictions on their killing, instituted penalties for liberating them, and legalized the use of poison for possum control[34]. However, this did not prevent possums from spreading. Occupying 54% of the country in 1950, their numbers raised to first 84% by 1963 and finally to 91% by 1980. In the early 2000s, there were possums almost everywhere throughout mainland New Zealand[35] with estimated numbers going up to 70 million[36].

4.2. The Multiple Impacts of Brushtail Possums

Possums as Herbivores

Brushtail possums were first recognized as pests in New Zealand because of their impacts as terrestrial and arboreal herbivores*. They are generalists and opportunistic folivores*, feeding on a wide range of leaves, flowers, fruits and other foods and have clear preferences for soft-leaved species (e.g. fuchsia*), although their diet typically consists primarily of the leaves of abundant canopy trees, such as kamahi (*Weinnmania racemosa*), southern rata*, pohutukawa (*Metrosideros excelsa*), Hall's totara (*Podocarpus hallii*), kohekohe (*Dysoxylum spectabile*) and tawa* *(Beilschmiedia tawa)*. In contrast, beech (*Nothofagus*), many ferns or subcanopy trees (as e.g. *Carpodetus serrata* or *Hedycarya arborea*) are not favoured by possums which is probably the reason why possum population densities are consequently much lower (approx. 1 ha^{-1}) in beech forests than in mixed lowland forests (5-10 ha^{-1}). Brushtail possums browse selectively through forests causing the depletion of some of the minor species named above as, for example fuchsia, in regions where possums are abundant[37].

Consuming 21,000 tonnes of vegetation a night[38], their impact is not restricted to foliage alone. In fact, they have

Fig. 9 *Forest dieback caused by brushtail possum invasion*

---

[34] Allen 266
[35] Possums
[36] Kiwi Conservation Club
[37] Allen 267
[38] Possums

been described as "reluctant folivores"[39], an assumption which is based on the fact that they achieve highest densities only in habitats where high-energy and nutrient-rich non-foliar foods such as fleshy fruits are seasonally abundant. In such habitats, their impacts on the vegetation are greater because their diet is still mainly foliage, resulting in the defoliation and decline of the most preferred species[40].

In spite of that, possums alone are rarely the ones to be responsible for changes in forest composition and structure. More often such changes come along with other agents, such as introduced deer or natural episodic events, like e.g. storm damage. Nevertheless, there are several examples of measured changes due to possum invasion with the worst occurring in forests in geologically unstable areas. Such forests tend to contain high proportions of shrubs and small trees and may, therefore, change relatively rapidly following possum invasion. A good example is the Adams River region (Westland) where an irrupting possum population defoliated or killed 50% of southern rata trees over a period of two years. The consequence of the reduction of the abundance of species preferred by possums is that less preferred species (such as *Hedycarya arborea* or *Alsophila* tree ferns) become more abundant leading to a change in the structure and composition of the forest's ecosystem[41].

Moreover, possums not only defoliate preferred species, but also suppress the fruiting of for example nikau palms* (*Rhopalostylis sapida*) and hinau* (*Elaeocarpus dentatus*) through their destruction of flower-bearing structures, flowers and developing fruits. A graphic illustration of the impacts of possums as herbivores is the rapid change in the health of preferred food species after possums have been reduced by control or eradicated which has recently been demonstrated for mistletoes on Kapiti Island[42].

Possums as Predators

Moreover, there is steadily accumulating evidence that possums can have serious impact as predators of native animals in New Zealand. As they are opportunistic feeders, their primarily herbivorous diet also consists of invertebrates, bird eggs and even nestlings when available. Insects (including fly larvae, stick insects, cicadas, weta* and beetles) have been recorded as regular components of possum diet in a wide range of habitats. That is why, in 1987, the biologists Cowan and Moeed

---

[39] Allen 267
[40] Allen 267
[41] Allen 267
[42] Allen 267

suggested that "large nocturnal insects such as weta, stag beetles and large weevils may become depleted where possums are abundant"[43]. In 2002, Dijkgraaf recorded consistently higher indices of weta abundance where possums had been controlled. However, this effect was confounded by a parallel reduction in rat abundance[44]; so, we cannot clearly state if possum control was the main cause.

Possums are increasingly recognized as significant nest predators, threatening the eggs and nestlings of a wide range of native birds such as kokako* (*Callaeas cinerea*), fantail (*Rhipidura fuliginosa*), Westland black petrel (*Procellaria westlandica*) and harrier (*Cirus approximans*). They have also been identified as predators of the eggs of kekeru (*Hemiphaga novaeseelandiae*), brown kiwi* (*Apteryx australis*) and kaka* (*Nestor meridionalis*). Although there is no evidence, it is very likely that nest predation by possums has been a significant factor in the decline of native birds such as kokako, and remains a limiting factor* for kekeru and other birds[45].

Despite of a lot of indices, it is difficult to separate the effects of possums on native fauna from those of rats or other introduced mammals, especially since possum and rat numbers are often reduced by the same management actions. In addition to specific evidence of predation, there are overall negative correlations of possum abundance and abundance of endemic species such as kaka, which is shown in the decline of vulnerable fauna like e.g. kaka and kokako in South Westland and Northland following possum invasions. Although the precise mechanisms involved may not be known (possibly a combination of predation and competition), the overall relationship is clear[46].

Possums as Competitors*

Several studies have highlighted the significant dietary overlap between possums and native birds such as kokako, making possums serious competitors concerning food resources. Frugivorous birds such as kokako and kekeru breed more frequently and successfully when large crops of fruit are available, and may not breed at all when fruit supplies are poor. It is also known that possums consume flowers, unripe fruit and ripe fruit, and severely reduce the fruit crops of nikau, hinau, tawa and other large-fruited species. Although there is no inevitable evidence, it is reasonable to

---

[43] Allen 268
[44] Allen 268
[45] Allen 268
[46] Allen 269

16

conclude that possums may affect the breeding success of frugivorous birds through competition for this key food source[47].

Another potential impact of possums on some native birds is competition for tree hollows or burrows. Possum require these for daytime dens, and some larger native birds (e.g. kaka or kiwi species) use similar-sized hollows or burrows for nesting and (in the case of the kiwi) also for daytime shelter. Individually possums typically use 5-10 dens within their home range, swapping them regularly. Use by a possum of the nest site of a bird during incubation or chick rearing is likely to be fatal for that nest, especially since predation of eggs or nestlings may occur as well. There have been records of instances of displacement of kiwi from burrows by possums, including one case in which a possum evidently killed an adult kiwi in a fight over burrow occupancy[48].

Possums as Seed Dispersers

The fact that possums consume a wide range of fleshy fruits suggests that they may also be important seed dispersers of native species. Although many of the seeds in fruits eaten by possums, especially larger, thin-coated ones such as tawa, are destroyed, there are still viable seeds of some species which can pass intact through the digestive tract and by being returned into soil, become again a fertile plant. However, the significance of possums as seed dispersers of native species in comparison to e.g. birds is strongly debated. Overall, the negative effects of possums on fruiting of native species such as nikau and hinau, and in destroying the thin-coated seeds of other species (as e.g. tawa) are likely to outweigh any potential benefits from seed dispersal[49].

Possums as Disease Vectors

Furthermore, possums are known to carry a range of diseases and endoparasites that can potentially infect humans and other animals. Especially bovine tuberculosis (Tb) is fatal to possums as it is prevalent in levels of 1-10% in possum populations in 28 discrete areas covering approx. 25% of New Zealand[50]. Tb infection of livestock (especially cattle and farmed deer) which occurs by environmental contamination and direct contact with dead or dying possums has dramatic effects on New

---

[47] Allen 269
[48] Allen 269
[49] Allen 270
[50] Allen 270

Zealand's cattle and sheep farming[51], the country's second most important industry. Beside the infection of wild mammals such as pigs and predators (e.g. ferrets) which is based mainly on the scavenging of possum carcasses, the rapid spread, the presence of bovine Tb in possums is the main reason why an eradication of this economically important disease is almost impossible[52] and occasions costs of $87 million (2006)[53].

According to Allen, a keystone species is a *"species whose effect is large, and disproportionately large relative to its abundance"*[54]. The effect of a species on its environment can be measured by the change in community characteristics as e.g. productivity or species richness of other members of the same ecosystem. If we take this definition as a basis, the brushtail possum is certainly a prime candidate for the title of a keystone alien species in many New Zealand forest communities, given the major ecological changes which have been recorded when possums have invaded or been removed from such communities. As the chart below shows, their food web connections reach lots of different species, from plants to almost all kinds of animals. They change forest composition by acting as herbivores and seed dispersers as well as the native fauna by acting as predators and competitors. In addition to their

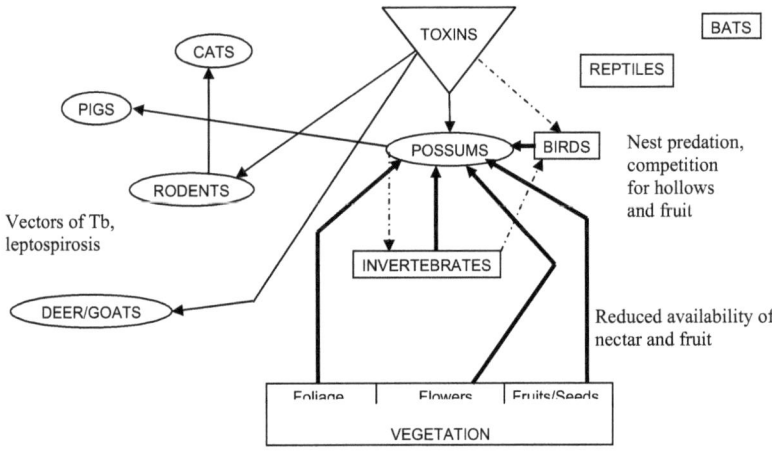

Fig. 10 *Impacts and food web connections of possums in New Zealand, and pathways of toxins used for their control*

---
[51] Opossums zerstören die Natur Neuseelands
[52] Allen 270
[53] Possums
[54] Allen 273

ecological effects and their role as disease vectors, control efforts such as poison used through non-target kills have dramatic effects on all other species related to possums in the sense of food web connections[55].

5. Pest Control – Preservation of Endemic Species

Looking at the effects of invasive species on the country's natural environment and regarding the fact that New Zealand has e.g. the highest rate of threatened bird species in the world (37 out of 50) it is quite obvious that there has to be done something to protect endemic biota. The first step on the way to protect native flora and fauna is to reduce the negative impact of aliens in order to restore natural resources and species which have and still are suffering from their introduction. This chapter will give insight into different methods of pest control as well as on restoration methods used by various both government and private societies who care about New Zealand's endemic biota and, therefore, do everything in order to protect it.

5.1. "Just a Dead Possum Is a Good Possum"[56] – Methods of Pest Control

Poisons

Having been in use since the 1950s, toxins in order to control introduced animals have a long tradition in New Zealand. Nowadays, sodium monofluoro-acetate or 1080 is the most common one used throughout the country. Usually being added to carrots, cereals or gel baits, it is then dropped by helicopters or airplanes in regions with high possum densities or where the terrain is too

Fig. 11 1080 carrots ready to be spread in Pureora Forest

difficult to use traps or to lay poison by hand. Being eaten by animals, 1080 causes their death within minutes through respiratory or cardiac failure[57].

However, most toxins used do not affect possums alone. Moreover, when being eaten by non-target animals, they have fatal consequences also on all other kinds of

---

[55] Allen 273
[56] Kölle
[57] Possums

terrestrial mammals – e.g. on other pests such as deer, stoats and rats but also on dogs (cf. fig. 10). There have been cases when dogs died of 1080 after having scavenged on possum carcasses, although owners are warned to keep their dogs away from poisoned areas[58]. In New Zealand, there is ongoing controversy about the use of 1080 for possum control. People oppose its use as they consider it inhumane and harmful to the environment as it also kills 'non-target' animals. Nevertheless, supporters claim that 1080 degrades in the environment, especially in water and that it does not persist in soil for more than a few weeks[59].

Harvesting

Another ongoing attempt by New Zealand industrialists is to reduce possum numbers by promoting possum harvesting. Coats made of possum fur or golf gloves made of possum leather are just some of the products which have always been popular. Moreover, possum meat is considered an aphrodisiac in Asia. However, prices for possum skins have dropped from 1987 onwards making New Zealand's possum export industry shrink to $35 million a year and making it almost impossible to live from possum hunting or fur trading[60].

Fig. 12 Coat made from possum fur

Being supported by the World Wildlife Fund New Zealand (WWFNZ) whose conservation director, Eric Pyle, states that they would "like to see all possums as dead possums"[61] and encourages the fur industry to "provide an additional incentive for people to kill possums"[62], companies are running programmes like printing "Thank you for buying possum fur. You are helping to save our

Fig. 13 Possum caught in a leg-hold trap

---

[58] Possums
[59] Possums
[60] Klotz
[61] Klotz
[62] Klotz

20

environment"[63] on products made of possums in order to appeal to the public to face the possum problem.

Trapping

Together with shooting of potential pests, trapping has the longest tradition in New Zealand. Initially used by trappers who were interested in catching an undamaged possum, it has been in use ever since. Today, there are many different types of traps which can be differentiated into two main groups: the ones where the possum stays alive (live trapping) and the ones where the possum is instantly killed.

Leg-hold traps, which are especially used by farmers to protect their stock from Tb, are often considered inhumane, as the possum caught stays alive and has to wait **Fig. 13** Possum caught in a leg-hold trap hours or even days for the farmer to come and shoot it. There are no initiatives where possums are liberated again, for example in different locations, after having been trapped as both the Department of Conservation and the Animal Health Board* consider killing as the only solution to the possum problem.

And this is exactly what the so-called Timms traps do, which can be bought from most agricultural suppliers. Being attracted by some food (apple, kiwifruit, orange, etc.) arranged in the yellow plastic box, the possum puts its head into the opening and triggers the striker rod, which instantly breaks its neck[64].

Fig. 14 Timms trap

Biotechnologies

A new approach to pest control is the use of new biotechnologies. With sciences such as molecular biology and genetic modification being developed and improved, methods such as fertility control of mammalian pests would be possible. Especially animals with a short life-span and a high potential reproductive rate, like e.g. stoats or possums, are excellent candidates for fertility control. Research has shown that possums treated with a new developed vaccine have reduced breeding by 70-80%. Therefore, reproduction control offers, in contrast to e.g. toxin, a humane and ethical method for managing pest species in New Zealand, and, when combined with conventional control, may provide a long-term and cost effective solution to the possum problem. Other advantages include decreasing the amount of toxin used, and

---

[63] Klotz
[64] Kiwi Conservation Club

21

thereby reducing the risk of environmental contamination as well as threats to non-target wildlife[65].

5.2. Restoration Methods used in New Zealand

Predator-Proof Fences

Since the 1950s, fences of varying designs have been used throughout the world to exclude predators from localized areas with high conservation values. Although their use in New Zealand has been limited so far, it is now increasing, initiated primarily by a growing interest in species restoration on the mainland. The probably best example is the 250-ha reserve at Karori on the outskirts of Wellington, which is currently the largest of its type. Its 8.6-km predator-proof fence protects a variety of

Fig. 15 Predator-proof fence at Tawharanui Regional Park

species which were formerly confined to offshore islands making it possible for the first time in more than a century that people in Wellington can "hear kiwi calling by night, and saddleback by day"[66].

In contrast to e.g. translocation attempts, projects involving predator-proof fences can also be a product of private or local initiatives, changing the public's attitude that wildlife management is the sole responsibility of government agencies[67]. Moreover, there is no doubt that the current interest in predator-proof fences will grow over the coming decades, although it is surprising that that they are not used more often nowadays to protect localized concentrations of threatened species, such as nesting waders on riverbeds, and seabirds in mainland habitats[68].

Translocation

Translocation – "the intentional release of a species in a new, safe location"[69] – is one of the main if not *the* main conservation strategy used in New Zealand,

---

[65] Allen 423
[66] Allen 373
[67] Allen 373
[68] Allen 374
[69] Allen 372

22

especially to save endangered bird species. By transferring them from the mainland (North Island, South Island or Stewart Island) to one of the many offshore islands surrounding New Zealand, the negative impact of predators can be removed and new populations can be established. In the period from 1992 to 1995 alone, there were at least 407 translocation events. Although many of them failed, others have been spectacularly successful and have saved many species from probable extinction, as it has e.g. the transfer of little spotted kiwi (*Apteryx owenii*) from South Island to Kapiti Island [70].

Parallel developments in techniques for eradicating potential predators, such as rats, cats, feral pigs, possums and stoats, make it possible to use previously infested islands for occupation by endangered wildlife. Such eradication programmes are now being attempted on large islands such as Kapiti ($20km^2$, 1996), Campbell ($113km^2$, 2001) and even on Rangitoto, a popular tourist highlight in the Hauraki Gulf about 30 minutes from Auckland Downtown. Estimations state that if technical advances continue at their present rate, even islands which are formidable challenges now could be cleared of e.g. rats within the next 20-50 years[71].

Since bird numbers doubled after removing possums between 1982 and 1988 from Kapiti Island (even though rats were still present)[72], translocation of endangered species in combination with eradication of predators seems to be an effective method of saving populations from getting extinct.

Breed in Captivity

Although the strategy of using captive-bred birds to establish self-sustaining population in the wild has had little success internationally, it turned out to be one of the most effective methods to protect and restore endangered bird species in New Zealand. The takahe* (*Porphyrio hochstetteri*) captive-rearing programme, which started in 1957, has contributed significantly to the survival of liberated populations and is one of the longest-running and most successful captive rearing programmes in the world. It has served as an example for numerous other endemic species, including kokako (*Callaeas cinerea*), kaka (*Nestor meridionalis*) and kiwi.

Especially used to protect some species from predators during brief but critical periods of life, such as e.g. breeding, new species are being added to the list of

---

[70] Allen 372
[71] Allen 373
[72] Possums

23

captive-bred birds each year, including several species of seabirds. This trend will continue, regarding the growing demand for founders to restock areas cleared of predators.

5.3. Advantages and Risks of Pest Control and Restoration Manage-ment Methods

Comparing the methods and projects named above it becomes clear that each of them has significant advantages, disadvantages or even risks, which will be worked out and evaluated throughout the following paragraphs.

Biotechnologies

The biggest advantage which comes along with the use of biotechnologies is the fact that no possum is killed. Reducing the population by preventing their breeding, it is considered the most humane pest control method.

However, with research being very expensive, development costs could be a limiting factor, being a handicap compared to relatively cheap traps or poison. Moreover, it will certainly take its time until proper vaccinations and technologies are ready to be used on a large scale, making biotechnologies more a method of the future than of the present.

Trapping

In contrast to biotechnologies, trapping offers a cheap but mainly ineffective method of possum control. Moreover, especially leg-hold traps are often considered inhumane, as a caught possum has to wait for somebody to shoot if not dying a slow and painful death. In addition, leg-hold traps installed on the ground pose a serious threat to terrestrial bird species like the kiwi, which is the reason why they are supposed to be put on tree trunks, bushes, etc. if possible.

Fig. 16 Bait station used in forests

Poison

The main problem posed by the use of poison like 1080 is the threat of non-target species and the risk of food-chain contamination. A suitable mean to reduce the

24

toxins influence on mammals is to put up so-called bait stations in regions which are frequently visited by humans or known to be often used by non-target species.

However, the use of 1080 is the most effective and probably only method available today with which the possum problem can fairly be handled.

Harvesting

The biggest advantage of harvesting same as for trapping is the fact that no poison is needed. Hence, it reduces contamination of soil and ground water and, moreover, minimizes the risk for other mammals to die of poison baits or the scavenging of poisoned possums.

Fig. 17 Possum skins drying

Although the fact that most possums are shot and skinned afterwards might seem crucial or inhumane, possum harvesting offers the chance of employment for hundreds of people as well as of boosting the country's export industry.

Captive-Breeding

As said before, captive-breeding is generally used to isolate threatened species for a short period of time. Although this might be an effective method to protect them, reintroduction problems following their liberation are common. Being excluded from their community, species who are dependant to live in a group have no chance to survive and will die pretty soon.

Moreover, the lack of genetic diversity which is prevalent in captive communities may not only cause genetic defects of potential descendants but also limit the grade to which a species can adapt to new surroundings and, therefore, contribute to their risk of probable extinction[73].

Translocation and Predator-Proof Fences

Being used to separate threatened species from potential predators, both translocation and predator-proof fences are considered highly ethical restoration methods.

Their main difference might be the fact that translocations are mainly of government concern, whereas predator-proof fences also offer the opportunity of private initiatives.

---

[73] Shah

The downside of translocations, however, is the eradication of predator species on 'translocation refuges' that often comes along with it, which is comparable to other pest control methods where pest species are killed.

Although some of the methods described above might seem to be inhumane and crucial it has turned out that possum control is essential and absolutely necessary if the possum problem should not get completely out of hand. In addition, the success of biodiversity regeneration after re-duction or removal of possums proves that New Zealand is on the right way.

Fig. 18 Mamaku tree recovering (two years after possum removal)

The next task for the people involved in pest control and restoration management will be to weigh the pros and cons and then decide which methods fit best and have the greatest chances of success.

6. Constant Dripping Wears the Stone – New Zealand in the 21st Century

Reading through my paper again, I think it is interesting to see what a big issue in all concerns pest control, the threat of aliens and the protection of endemic species is for New Zealand. Even though I thought I knew a lot about the country it was astonishing for me see to what you do not get to know as a tourist and compare it to things which are apparent. Having been at many of the places and locations mentioned above, it was quite easy for me to identify with the things I found out and to associate them with the corresponding pictures of landscapes and nature.

Having done the first step by realizing the threats and problems caused by allegedly harmless animals or even pets, the youngest country on earth is now being confronted with the challenge of finding suitable means to protect their native biodiversity. This process will certainly continue for the next decades even with progress especially concerning biotechnologies being achieved relatively fast. New methods will be developed and new opportunities will be provided. The main question will be: will New Zealand be able to win a fight against a world which will become smaller and smaller, where it will be possible to cover even huge distances in almost no time and where increasing international travelling and trade will make it easier and easier for invasive species to come to the country? Or will probably New Zealand's biggest industry interfere because limitation *of* or strict rules *for* people coming to the country in order to minimize the risk of invasions cannot be in the interest of people being involved in tourism and making money from people visiting the country?

7. Appendix

7.1. The Brushtail Possum – A Brief Description[74]

Physical Description

Body Length:	320-580 mm
Tail Length:	240-350 mm
Weight:	2–4kg
Fur:	short but dense
Ears:	tall and rounded
Tail:	typically long, covered in long bushy fur
Coat colours:	grey, black, red (varying according to habitat), lighter on the underside
5 Subspecies in Australia:	*T.v. vulpecula* (found in southern Australia, grey)
	T.v. arnhemensis (northern regions of Australia, grey)
	T.v. eburacensis (Cape York, grey)
	T.v. johnsoni (eastern Queensland, red)
	T.v. fuliginosus (Tasmania, black)

Reproduction

Two breeding seasons:	spring and autumn; but females usually give birth only once a year (1 young)
Oestrous cycle[*]:	approx. 25 days
Gestation period[*]:	approx. 18 days

---

[74] Trichosurus Vulpecula

Weight at birth:	approx. 1g
Time in pouch:	approx. 4 months
Weaned:	after 6 months
Leaving mother:	after 8-18 months
Sexual maturity:	females after 12 months, males after 2 years
Average life-span:	7 years (in the wild) – 14 years (captivity)

Behaviour

Trichosurus vulpecula is an arboreal, nocturnal animal, which means that during daytime it rests in hollowed out logs or trees. In urban areas it can also be found in peoples' attics.

Being a solitary species, they mark their territories using anal secretions as well as secretions from the scent gland on their chests. Nevertheless, as they are so abundant, many individuals' home ranges overlap. There seems too be, however, little direct aggression between individuals. Guttural vocalizations are used either to communicate territory location or to attract mates during breeding season.

Although they do not live in groups, clear dominance hierarchies exist where co-dominants of the same sex purposely avoid another, i.e. where territories overlap.

Distribution

Trichosurus vulpecula has the widest distribution of any Australian mammal, as it can be found in most of Australia and Tasmania. Additionally, it was introduced to New Zealand in 1837.

Habitat

Brushtail possums mainly reside in wooded or forested areas as they provide the kind of food they need. However, they can vary greatly throughout its range. Living in rain-forests as for example in Tasmania, they can also be seen in dry woodland areas. In New Zealand, they can be found in most forested areas.

Food Habits

Although the brushtail possum mainly feeds on a wide range of leaves, shoots, flowers and fruits, its diet also consists of insects, snails, eggs or even small chicks (cf. chapter 4.2).

7.2. Glossary

Term	*Explanation*
Animal Health Board	The Animal Health Board is a "non-profit making incorporate society, made up of representatives from the farming sector and local government"[75] whose mission is to "eradicate bovine tuberculosis (Tb) from New Zealand, on order to protect New Zealand's access to export markets for dairy, beef and deer products"[76].
Arboreal	living in trees
Biodiversity	"'biological diversity' [is defined as] the number and variety of organisms found within a specified geographic region; and the variability among living organisms on earth, including the variability within and between species and within and between ecosystems"[77].
Canopy	"The canopy is one of the uppermost levels of a forest, below the emergent layer, formed by the tree crowns"[78].
Carnivore	"A carnivore [...] is any animal with a diet consisting mainly of meat, whether it comes from animals living (predation) or dead (scavenging)"[79].
Competition	The "use of the same limited resource by two or more species"[80].
Department of Conservation	"The Department of Conservation (In Maori, *Te Papa Atawhai*) [...] is the state sector organisation of New Zealand which deals with the conservation of New Zealand's natural and historic heritage. [...] This includes preservation of historic sites on public conservation land, saving native threatened species, managing threats like pests and weeds, environmental restoration, caring for marine life, and assisting landowners to effectively preserve natural heritage"[81].
Ecosystem	"An ecosystem is a natural unit consisting of all plants, animals

---

[75] Animal Health Board
[76] Animal Health Board
[77] New Zealand Biodiversity
[78] Canopy
[79] Carnivore
[80] Competition
[81] Department of Conservation

	and micro-organisms (biotic factors) in an area functioning together with all of the non-living physical (abiotic) factors of the environment"[82] like e.g. temperature, precipitation, humidity, etc.
Folivore	A folivore is a herbivore that specializes in eating leaves"[83]
Food chain/ food web	Food chains describe the eating relationship between species within an ecosystem. A food web extends the linear concept of the food chain to a complex network of interactions. This is necessary as most consumers feed on more than one species and are, in turn, fed upon by multiple other species[84].
Gestation period	"the period during which an embryo develops"[85]
Herbivore	"A herbivore is an animal that is adapted to eat plants and no meat"[86].
Limiting factor	"A limiting factor or limiting resource is one that controls a process, such as organism growth or species population size or distribution. The availability of food, predation pressure, or availability of shelter are examples of factors that could be limiting for an organism"[87].
Monotype	A "monotype is a taxonomic group* with only one type"[88], e.g. a genus which has only one species.
Mustelid	member of the weasel family
Nocturnal	active at night
Oestrous cycle	The oestrous cycle "comprises the recurring physiologic changes that are induced by reproductive hormones in most mammalian [but not human] placental females"[89].
Omnivore	"Omnivores are species that eat both plants and animals as their primary food source"[90].
Taxonomic	Taxonomic groups or taxonomic ranks are used for biological

---

[82] Ecosystem
[83] Folivore
[84] Food chain
[85] Gestation period
[86] Herbivore
[87] Limiting factor
[88] Monotype
[89] Oestrous cycle
[90] Omnivore

group	classification in order to express relationships between species, families, etc. Nowadays, we distinguish eight major taxonomic ranks in the following hierarchical order: Life, Domain, Kingdom, Phylum, Class, Order, Family, Genus and Species.
Terrestrial	living on or relating on land rather than water[91]

7.3. Endemic New Zealand Biota Mentioned

Fig. 19	Fig. 20
Fuchsia *Aristotelia serrata*	**Hinau** *Elaeocarpus dentatus*
Fig. 21	Fig. 22
Kaka, North Island *Nestor meridionalis*	**Kauri Tree** *Agathis australis*

[91] Terrestrial

Fig. 23	Fig. 24
Kiwi, North Island Brown *Apteryx australis*	**Kokako** *Callaeas cinera*
Fig. 25	Fig. 26
Nikau Palm Tree *Rhopalostylis sapida*	**Petrel**, Westland Black *Procellaria westlandica*
Fig. 27	Fig. 28
Pingao Golden Sand Sedge *Desmoschoenus spiralis*	**Rata Tree,** Southern *Metrosideros umbellata*
Fig. 29	Fig. 30
Takahe	**Tawa**

32

Porphyrio hostetteri	*Beilschmiedia tawa*
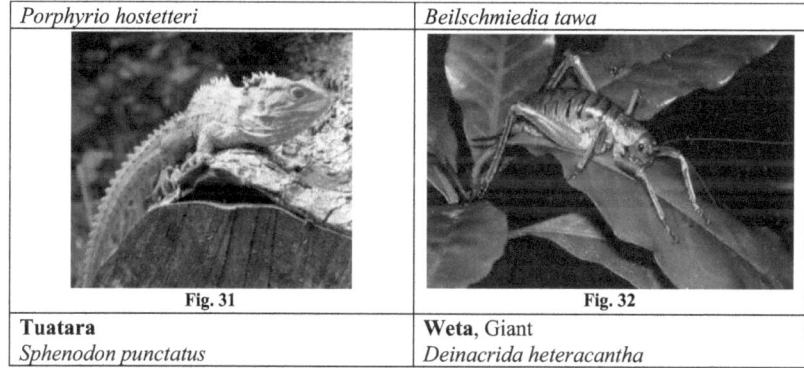 Fig. 31	Fig. 32
Tuatara *Sphenodon punctatus*	**Weta**, Giant *Deinacrida heteracantha*

8. Works Cited

Books:

Allen, Dr. Robert B. *Biological Invasions in New Zealand*. Berlin/Heidelberg: Springer-Verlag, 2006

Darby, John. *Natural History of Southern New Zealand*. Dunedin: University of Otago Press, 2003

McDowall, R.M. *Gamekeepers for the Nation: The Story of New Zealand's Acclimati-sation Societies 1861-1990*. Christchurch: Canterbury University Press, 1994

Articles:

Duffy, Dr. J. Emmet. "Biodiversity".
<http://www.eoearth.org/article/Biodiversity> September 21, 2008

Klotz, Hattie. "Fur Fashion to the Rescue". Adapted from *The Ottawa Citizen*.
<http://tinyurl.com/ax7grs> January 20, 2009

Kölle, Ingrid. "Beuteltiere raus – Artenschutz in Neuseeland".
<http://tinyurl.com/5afjhs> September 6, 2008

McGinley, Mark. "Biological diversity in New Zealand".
<http://tinyurl.com/czml78> September 6, 2008

"Opossums zerstören die Natur Neuseelands". Adapted from *WWF Neuseeland*, September 1999. <http://tinyurl.com/dyzjar> October 26, 2008

Shah, Anup. "Why Is Biodiversity Important? Who Cares?"
<http://tinyurl.com/cb5ohj> January 22, 2009

Internet:

"Bream Head Conservation Trust".
<http://www.breamheadtrust.org.nz/vision.php> January 18, 2009

Conservation International. "Biodiversity Hotspots".
<http://tinyurl.com/4tazmm> September 28, 2008

Kiwi Conservation Club. "Possum Control".
<http://www.kcc.org.nz/pests/possum/control.asp> November 28, 2008

"New Zealand Biodiversity".
<http://tinyurl.com/akc8lh> September 28, 2008

"Possums". Adapted from *Te Ara: The Encyclopedia of New Zealand*.
<http://tinyurl.com/6hbr9y> November 28, 2008

"Trichosurus Vulpecula". Retrieved from *Encyclopedia of Life*.
<http://tinyurl.com/cjdont> October 26, 2008

Definitions:

"Canopy". Adapted from *Wikipedia, the free encyclopedia*.
<http://en.wikipedia.org/wiki/Canopy_(forest)> January 18, 2008

"Carnivore". Adapted from *Wikipedia, the free encyclopedia*.
<http://en.wikipedia.org/wiki/Carnivore> November 7, 2008

"Competition". Adapted from *Biology Online*.
<http://www.biology-online.org/dictionary/Competition> January 21, 2009

"Department of Conservation". Adapted from *Wikipedia, the free encyclopedia*.
<http://en.wikipedia.org/wiki/Department_of_Conservation> November 30,
2008

"Ecosystem". Adapted from *Wikipedia, the free encyclopedia*.
<http://en.wikipedia.org/wiki/Ecosystem> October 25, 2008

"Folivore". Adapted from *Wikipedia, the free encyclopedia*.
<http://en.wikipedia.org/wiki/Folivore> December 31, 2008

"Food chain". Adapted from *Wikipedia, the free encyclopedia*.
<http://en.wikipedia.org/wiki/Food_chain> October 25, 2008

"Gestation period".
<http://dictionary.die.net/gestation%20period> January 25, 2009

"Haast's Eagle". Adapted from *Wikipedia, the free encyclopedia*.
<http://en.wikipedia.org/wiki/Harpagornis> October 18, 2008

"Herbivore". Adapted from *Wikipedia, the free encyclopedia*.
<http://en.wikipedia.org/wiki/Herbivore> November 7, 2008

"Limiting factor". Adapted from *Wikipedia, the free encyclopedia*.
<http://en.wikipedia.org/wiki/Limiting_factor> November 25, 2008

"Omnivore". Adapted from *Wikipedia, the free encyclopedia*.
<http://en.wikipedia.org/wiki/Omnivore> November 7, 2008

"Terrestrial". Retrieved from *LDOCE Online*.
<http://www.ldoceonline.com/dictionary/terrestrial> October 26, 2008

9. List of Figures

Fig. 17 *Possum skins drying.*
<http:/tinyurl.com/bkcegf> January 24, 2009

Fig. 18 *Mamaku tree recovering (two years after possum removal).*
<http:/tinyurl.com/dlmgjt> January 25, 2009

Fig. 19 *Fuchsia.*
<http://www.arthurleej.com/images/Aristo.jpg> November 25, 2008

Fig. 20 *Hinau.*
<http:/tinyurl.com/aah2qn> January 25, 2009

Fig. 21 *Kaka, North Island.*
<http://www.parrot.co.nz/Parrot.Images/kaka1.jpg> November 8, 2008

Fig. 22 *Kauri Tree.*
<http://www.priskaunddavid.ch/pics/Kauri2.JPG > January 25, 2009

Fig. 23 *Kiwi, North Island Brown.*
<http://tinyurl.com/69m93z> November 8, 2008

Fig. 24 *Kokako.*
<http://tinyurl.com/5wq5z5> November 25, 2008

Fig. 25 *Nikau Palm Tree.*
<http://www.neotropic.com/images/rhop_sap1.JPG> October 19, 2008

Fig. 26 *Petrel, Westland Black.*
<http://www.tommy777.addr.com/Westland_Petrel.jpg> January 25, 2009

Fig. 27 *Pingao Golden Sand Sedge.*
<http://tinyurl.com/6elgu4> September 28, 2008

Fig. 28 *Rata Tree, Southern.*
<http://www.bdtravels.com/K06x.jpg> October 26, 2008

Fig. 29 *Takahe.*
<http://www.thevinery.co.uk/images/nature/takahe.jpg> January 25, 2009

Fig. 30 *Tawa.*
<http://tinyurl.com/6ehzux> October 19, 2008

Fig. 31 *Tuatara.*
<http://tinyurl.com/5q4t9z> November 23, 2008

Fig. 32 *Weta, Giant.*
<http://www.doc.govt.nz/upload/225/weta.jpg> November 8, 2008

YOUR KNOWLEDGE HAS VALUE

- We will publish your bachelor's and master's thesis, essays and papers

- Your own eBook and book - sold worldwide in all relevant shops

- Earn money with each sale

Upload your text at www.GRIN.com
and publish for free